Managing Change at Work

Leading People Through Organizational T

Third Edition

Cynthia D. Scott, Ph.D., M.P.H. and Dennis T. Jaffe, Ph.D.

A Crisp Fifty-Minute™ Series Book

This Fifty-Minute™ book is designed to be "read with a pencil." It is an excellent workbook for self-study as well as classroom learning. All material is copyright-protected and cannot be duplicated without permission from the publisher. *Therefore, be sure to order a copy for every training participant by contacting:*

THOMSON

COURSE TECHNOLOGY ™

1-800-442-7477 • 25 Thomson Place, Boston MA • www.courseilt.com

Managing Change at Work

Leading People Through Organizational Transitions

Third Edition

**Cynthia D. Scott, Ph.D., M.P.H. and
Dennis T. Jaffe, Ph.D.**

CREDITS:
Senior Editor: **Debbie Woodbury**
Editor: **Ann Gosch**
Assistant Editor: **Genevieve McDermott**
Production Manager: **Denise Powers**
Design: **Nicole Phillips**
Production Artist: **Rich Lehl**
Cartoonist: **Ralph Mapson**

ISBN 1-56052-692-0
Library of Congress Catalog Card Number 2003115408
Printed in Canada by Webcom Limited
3 4 5 PM 06 05

Learning Objectives For:

MANAGING CHANGE AT WORK

The objectives for *Managing Change at Work, Third Edition* are listed below. They have been developed to guide you, the reader, to the core issues covered in this book.

THE OBJECTIVES OF THIS BOOK ARE:

❑ 1) To explore changes taking place in organizations today

❑ 2) To explain how organizations can prepare for change

❑ 3) To clarify human reactions to change and how to deal with them

❑ 4) To explain team involvement and visionary leadership

ASSESSING YOUR PROGRESS

In addition to the learning objectives above, Course Technology has developed a Crisp Series **assessment** that covers the fundamental information presented in this book. A 25-item, multiple-choice and true/false questionnaire allows the reader to evaluate his or her comprehension of the subject matter. To buy the assessment and answer key, go to www.courseilt.com and search on the book title or via the assessment format, or call 1-800-442-7477.

Assessments should not be used in any employee selection process.

About the Authors

Cynthia D. Scott, Ph.D., M.P.H., is a founding partner of Changeworks Global. She is a recognized leader in the fields of change leadership, executive development, and knowledge mobilization. She consults with organizations on managing organizational change, building resilient cultures, and executive team development. She earned her M.P.H. in health planning at the University of Michigan and her Ph.D. in psychology at The Fielding Institute. She is a licensed clinical psychologist.

Dennis T. Jaffe, Ph.D., is professor and director of the Organizational Inquiry Program at Saybrook Graduate School in San Francisco and a founding partner of Changeworks Global. He is nationally recognized in the fields of executive team development, family business transitions, and organizational assessment. He consults with organizations on managing organizational change, long-range planning, and designing collaborative workplaces. He earned his M.A. degree in management and his Ph.D. in sociology at Yale.

Drs. Jaffe and Scott have written 10 books including *Getting Your Organization to Change, Rekindling Commitment, Take This Work and Love It, Empowerment, Organizational Mission, Vision, and Values,* and *Mastering the Change Curve Assessment.* Their high content keynotes on *Change Leadership, Navigating the Global Work Environment,* and *Building Career Readiness* have provided an exciting and stimulating foundation for employees to engage in change. They have co-designed training and assessment tools, including Organizational Readiness Assessment and Leading for Results. Their video, *Managing People Through Change,* was selected as one of the best of 1990 by *Human Resource Executive.*

Changeworks Global (www.changeworksglobal.com) is a San Francisco-based consulting firm where Dr. Scott and Dr. Jaffe design and provide consultation to implement outcome-oriented change-management solutions with leadership teams. They have worked with a wide range of clients worldwide on mergers, technology implementations, cultural transformations, and organizational re-design.

Leading Change at Work^SM and Change Mastery^SM are two interactive workshops that have assisted thousands of managers and employees to learn the skills they need to manage and lead change. Changeworks Global offers train-the-trainer, online, and customized tool kits for large group applications.

Changeworks Global
461 Second St. #232
San Francisco, CA 94117
(415) 546-4488
cscott@changeworksglobal.com

How to Use This Book

This *Fifty-Minute™ Series Book* is a unique, user-friendly product. As you read through the material, you will quickly experience the interactive nature of the book. There are numerous exercises, real-world case studies, and examples that invite your opinion, as well as checklists, tips, and concise summaries that reinforce your understanding of the concepts presented.

A Crisp Learning *Fifty-Minute™ Book* can be used in a variety of ways. Individual self-study is one of the most common. However, many organizations use *Fifty-Minute* books for pre-study before a classroom training session. Other organizations use the books as a part of a systemwide learning program—supported by video and other media based on the content in the books. Still others work with Crisp Learning to customize the material to meet their specific needs and reflect their culture. Regardless of how it is used, we hope you will join the more than 20 million satisfied learners worldwide who have completed a *Fifty-Minute Book*.

Preface

"
The present is a time of great entrepreneurial ferment, where old and staid institutions suddenly have to become very limber."

—Peter Drucker

Change in the workplace has become a way of life. Mergers, layoffs, deregulation, growth, re-organization, new technology, and increased competition are daily occurrences. As a manager and leader, you are challenged to maintain performance under chaotic, complex conditions. Your job is to keep your team focused, engaged, and productive in the midst of re-setting expectations about rewards, career development, and organizational strategy. This book will help you build a motivated and productive workforce.

➤ Understand your role in leading the changing workplace

➤ Set a vision with your group

➤ Lead organizational culture change

➤ Understand and manage people through change

➤ Provide change leadership

➤ Deal with individual and group resistance

➤ Negotiate new work arrangements

➤ Avoid common pitfalls

Since we first published this book more than 10 years ago, the field of change management has exploded and everyone has become a "change consultant." As key thought leaders in the field, we are delighted to continue to share our recent thinking to support employees, managers, and organizations to achieve high performance. In our continuing experience with leaders who are working to transform their organizations, we have found the core principles in this book to endure.

In this revised edition we have provided our point of view on the competencies you will need to be a change leader in the future. This book will give you step-by-step advice and activities to become an effective change leader in your organization.

Good Luck!

Cynthia D. Scott, Ph.D., M.P.H.   Dennis T. Jaffe, Ph.D.

Contents

Part 3: Leading Change

Part 4: Creating a Change Action Plan

INTRODUCTION

2

Getting the Most from This Book

Creating sustainable workplace change is often challenging and complex. Yet there has been only slight focus by most organizations on the management of human capital through periods of change. A classic book on mergers and acquisitions devotes only four pages to what to do with the people in the organization during periods of change.

Many companies have discovered that although they have moved the desks, they have not moved the "hearts" of the employees who work there. When this happens, management is often frustrated by resistance and lack of productivity among the workforce. This book provides strategies and skills that will help managers develop the core competency of change management.

Each change is unique and requires a customized approach to ensure positive outcomes. There is no single, foolproof list of steps. Depending on the situation, as a manager you must customize and experiment. The following model provides a "big picture" of the levels at which change needs to be managed and some of the high level phases along each path. You can use this to help organize your overall approach to managing change. For a more in-depth explanation of this model see *Getting Your Organization to Change,* ©1999. Each change requires adaptation of this framework to your situation. Use it as a guide to turn your ideas into strategies and actions.

Organizational Components	Change Management Phases		
	Assess & Mobilize	**Design the Changes**	**Implement the Transformation**
Level One *Top Leadership* (Sponsor/Executive Team)	*Align Top Leadership*	*Make the Case for Change*	*Champion New Ways*
Level Two *Change Team* (Change Leader & Change Navigator)	*Convene and Charter the Change Team*	*Design New Processes*	*Cascade Change Leadership*
Level Three *Employee Involvement* (Team Members/ Stakeholders)	*Develop Individual Change Capabilities*	*Employee Involvement Process*	*Develop New Teams*
Level Four *Organizational Culture & Change Processes* (All)	*Assess Organizational Change Capabilities*	*Align Systems with New Processes*	*Anchor Organizational Learning*

Assumptions About Change

Over the years of working with hundreds of leaders and organizations, we have found that we share the same basic thoughts about creating and managing change. This is the list we use to guide our approach.

➤ Change can begin anywhere.

➤ Everyone is responsible for making change work.

➤ There is never enough information.

➤ There is no quick fix.

➤ Change is both toxic and tonic.

➤ Change requires exchange and communication.

➤ Change is stressless only for the mindless.

➤ Change challenges people in power.

➤ Change makes everyone restless.

1

Facing Change

> "*Warned of impending upheaval, most managers still pursue business as usual. Yet business as usual is dangerous in an environment that has become, for all practical purposes, permanently convulsive.*"

–**Alvin Toffler,** ***The Adaptive Corporation***

The Pace of Organizational Change

In recent years global trends have broadly impacted organizations. Although the specifics may vary, change is happening in more workplaces and at a faster rate. The reasons are not just "flavor of the month." They are in response to an increasing need for flexibility, productivity, shifting strategy, and leadership changes. Traditionally, change was experienced in short bursts of disruption followed by a longer period of stable operations. Today there are no longer any rest periods; change is experienced in a continuous and pervasive manner requiring constant adaptation.

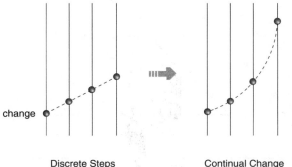

Discrete Steps   Continual Change

The pace of organizational change is increasing. Recent studies show that:

➤ More than 61 million Americans will retire in the next 30 years

➤ 32% of workers say they will likely change jobs within the next five years

➤ White males are a minority in the U.S. workplace

➤ Women make up 60% of the U.S. workforce, and the percentage is growing

➤ Huge productivity gains are needed to remain competitive

➤ 40% of the U.S. workforce was unionized 40 years ago—now it is less than 5%

➤ 70% of mergers end up as financial failures

Where to Focus Your Efforts

When 5% of the people in a group adopt a change, the change is *imbedded*. When 20% adopt it, the change is *unstoppable*. Once you get the innovators and early adopters on board, the success of your change is more assured.

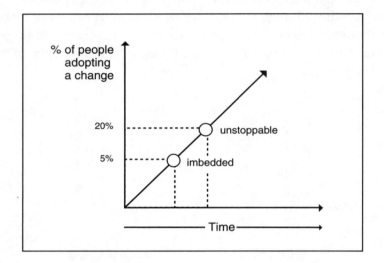

People adapt to change at different rates. *Innovators* try things first, and then *early adopters* follow their lead. It is important to focus on these two groups to build momentum for change. Hopefully, with support and encouragement, the rest of the organization will follow. Some people will find it very hard to change; they may experience too much risk and loss, either in skill, status, or identity. It is important to support people who are having a hard time; they may have important knowledge that can increase innovation.

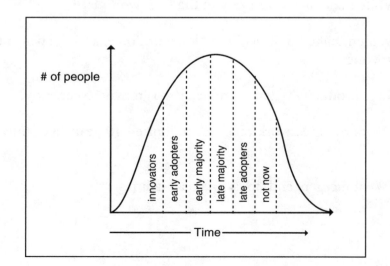

WHAT CHANGES HAVE YOU EXPERIENCED?

Take a moment to assess the changes you have faced in the last two years.

1 = not much

2 = some disruption

3 = a lot of disruption

CHANGE	IMPACT OF CHANGE		
	1	2	3
Technology			
Demand for higher productivity			
Change in benefits/retirement plan			
Outsourcing			
Layoffs/downsizing			
Start-up of new division or company			
Leadership changes			
Culture change—new policies, values, expectations			
Major re-orginization (merger, spinoff)			
Serious and new competitors			
Add your own personal /family or life event changes:			

Managing in Today's Changing Organization

In the last century the definition of management competence rested on specific planning, scheduling, and controlling techniques. Today managerial/leadership competence is based on the ability to create sustainable improvements in innovation and productivity. The ability to manage and create change is a core competency for success in today's organizations. Today's managers must be change managers or, as this book recommends, change *leaders*.

Change leadership is not a skill reserved just for top management. As organizations struggle to respond to the pressures of competition, including the global business environment, you and your work team must learn to move quickly to attain higher standards and increased productivity. If you do not succeed, your organization may not survive.

Organizational Changes

To respond to a complex, global marketplace, organizations today ask each individual to take more responsibility and accountability. The structure of some organizations becomes flatter and less hierarchical—emphasizing self-management and teamwork to support constant adaptation and constant innovation.

In short, an organization with a future in today's changing environment possesses the following characteristics:

➤ Learning orientation—search for best practices

➤ Relationship focus—among the employees and the customers

➤ Constant innovation—rejuvenation, breakthrough ideas/products/ services

➤ Flexibility—responsiveness to customers, employees

➤ Knowledge mobilization—gathering what everyone knows and applying it to increase productivity

➤ Emotional literacy—creating "community" in the workplace

Signs of Workplace Change

As organizations adapt to increased demand for productivity and performance they often adopt policies that increase the amount of choice, involvement, and participation that employees have. This tends to "buffer" the higher demand. Below are some of the ways organizations can change.

➤ More employee involvement in all levels of decision making

➤ Increased emphasis on "meaningful work"

➤ More responsibility and accountability for individual employees

➤ Fewer managers and increased emphasis on self-managing teams

➤ A flatter process-focused organizational structure

➤ People responsible for their own skill development

➤ A focus on human capital as demonstrated by an investment in training, retraining, and new skill development

➤ An atmosphere that encourages more mutual respect and trust

➤ Free agents—outsourced employees

➤ Emphasis on supporting work and family balance

➤ Increased encouragement of learning and creativity away from the workplace via tuition and fee reimbursement plans

➤ Better recognition and reward for superior performance

➤ Anytime, anyplace workplaces (telecommuting)

➤ Greater diversity in the workforce with more women and minorities

The Importance of Continuous Learning

In a constantly changing organization, no set of skills stays useful forever. The technical skills a person learns in school or on the job quickly become obsolete. Today it is important to adjust your expectations to include continuous learning.

Seeing Your Work in a New Way

To be successful today, people have to master a wide range of new skills often and quickly. They have to be open to changing old ways of doing things to learn new tasks and adopt new skills. The ability to evolve with the new workplace requires a new way of seeing your work as follows:

➤ Every employee will have to take greater responsibility. In their best-selling book, *Take This Job and Love It**, the authors call this the "two-job concept." Besides handling their regular jobs, employees have a "second job" of helping the organization change and continuously improve.

➤ It is no longer possible for a company to guarantee an employee a specific job. If individuals want to remain with an organization, they will have to learn to master many jobs and continually expect to shift. Often this will be not just in one department or specialty, but broadly, such as from manufacturing to marketing or from technical engineering to sales. The most valuable employees will be the ones with the flexibility to master the most challenges.

➤ Organizations are networks—focused on ever-changing customer demand and marketplace needs. Information will have to be broadly shared, because more groups will need it. As a manager, your role will shift away from the traditional role of controlling, to keeping your team focused, aligned, trained, and flexible to accomplish continually changing goals.

**Take This Job and Love It,* Simon & Schuster, New York, 1988. Revised and reissued as *Take This Work and Love It,* Crisp Publications, 1997.

Organizational Responses to Change

Change creates pressure in any organization. There is a cognitive, emotional, and structural gap between what currently exists and what is planned. The management of this tension, with planning and implementation efforts, is the core of successful change management. Different parts of the organization respond to this tension in different ways.

Top Management

Leaders often underestimate the impact that change has on their employees. As visionaries, their role is to engage in strategic planning sessions in relation to the changing environment. Because of this focus, they often think that communicating the new direction gives everyone an understanding of the strategy. They downplay the need to mobilize their organization and often expect employees to "go along" when a change is announced and blame their middle managers if people resist or complain about the change. They often feel betrayed when employees do not respond positively.

Middle Management

Managers in the middle feel the pressure to "make the organization change" according to the vision of top management. They feel pulled in different directions. Middle managers often lack the information and leadership direction needed to focus when confronted with multiple priorities. They are caught in the middle balancing multiple priorities because they do not have a clear view to make sense of complex situations. They are often besieged with upset, resistant, or withdrawn employees who no longer respond to prior management approaches, and they feel deserted, blamed, or misunderstood by their leaders.

Employees/Workers/Associates

Workers often feel attacked and betrayed by changes announced by management. They are often caught off guard. Their resistance is often heightened because they have not been part of understanding the changing environment and the planning process. Many respond with resistance, anger, frustration, and confusion. Their response can solidify into a wall of "retirement on the job." They become afraid to take risks or try new things. They experience a loss of traditional relationships, familiar structure, and predictable career advancement patterns.

The Leader's Role During Change

In times of change, every manager, supervisor, and team leader will be called upon to lead change in their groups. Top management should not be expected to manage the transition of individual work groups. Many middle managers wait for their leaders to tell them what to do, but communication between top executives and middle managers often is poor and there is no strategy to effectively announce and implement change.

Managers want answers. When there are no ready solutions, they often blame top management for leaving them in the dark. The best advice for these managers is to stop waiting and start leading their teams. If you sit around waiting, the wave of change may wash over you and drown you. To stay afloat you must learn to manage change.

Change offers managers both uncertainty and opportunity. How you manage yourself and your work groups will make all the difference. By following the steps and strategies in this book, you can learn how to view change as an opportunity and create a culture of productivity and growth.

The Changing Organizational Culture

You cannot change a culture by itself, because a culture does not exist by itself. It is "held" in new patterns of work, reporting relationships, decision-making, leadership, product focus, customer expectations, and so on. Changing any of these affects the way people are accustomed to doing things and requires people to let go of "how it was" and move through a period of doubt and uncertainty.

Managers must understand that these changes in any of the above areas will disturb the culture and require management involvement. The ability of managers to predict, acknowledge, and assist people through these transitions requires a special set of skills outlined in this book. Organizations that effectively handle changing an organization's culture will reduce the time required for similar changes in the future.

Helping Yourself to Be a Better Change Leader

You cannot escape or hide from organizational change. It comes with the territory. Problems come when people are not allowed to manage the change and are not taught the skills to learn how to learn. For an organization to adapt to change, you must help your group move through change. And helping yourself through change is an important part of being a change leader. *Managing Personal Change*,* by the authors of this book, focuses on the skills needed to complete a personal transition successfully.

Going through any major change will challenge the way you view yourself. Major changes can be like the death and rebirth of a company. Living through this process is similar to a major kitchen remodel. To obtain the result you want, you first must rip out the old kitchen, leaving a basic structure and emptiness. Then you begin to bring in new cabinets and appliances that fit coherently. Once you add the final touches, you can move back in and feel comfortable and productive again. And like any remodeling project, it always takes longer than you thought and costs more than you estimated!

**Managing Personal Change,* Crisp Publications.

Five Elements to Change Planning

You may not know when a change is in the works, but when it happens, you are far from helpless. Although much may be beyond your control, you can anticipate and influence many aspects of implementing change. Begin change management by using the Change Planning Tool. Involve your group as soon as possible to move them smoothly through change. In effective organizations, people share basic goals and communicate clearly, directly, and regularly about what they are doing. During change, exercise leadership through vision, coordination, and facilitation. Together, you and your group can make things happen.

Change Planning Tool				
Relationship	**Culture**	**Stakeholder**	**Structure**	**Information**
Where Leader Focuses Attention Attitudes, needs, and motivations, development, interactions, work relations, commitment	Meaning, values, purpose, norms, vision, rituals	Politics, power, stakeholders, interests, fears, concerns, personal and group agendas	Goals, roles, tasks, work processes, resources, reporting responsibility	Feedback processes, matrices, information flow, data, technology networks, access, choices
Leader Actions Dealing with resistance, encouraging communication, supporting people during change	Helping people develop a new purpose and vision they can believe in, shifting to new ways	Aligning agendas, balancing interests to reduce concerns and conflict, building coalitions among those with a stake in results	Clarifying goals, roles, core processes, boundaries, rules, decision making	Locating and providing reliable data and feedback to support decisions, measure and improve performance
Key Words Commitment Involvement Teamwork Motivation Morale	Vision Heroes Values Meaning	Power Politics Interests Alignment Agenda	Roles Responsibility Decision making Levels Boundaries	Big picture Rewards Measures Performance management
Key Leader Tasks Communicate need for change Listen to concerns Hold change meetings Build participation	Generate vision Define values Challenge norms Design symbolic actions and events	Engage stakeholders Organize stakeholder gatherings and councils Negotiate support	Role contracting Process design Set clear decision making levels Clarify boundaries	Allow access to all information Create information dashboards Give reward for performance Give feedback on results

As a manager you have special responsibilities to maintain strong upward linkage between strategic and operational levels in the organization. If you keep the information you receive from above to yourself, or if you feel you are the only one who knows how to handle change, your controlling leadership will not be helpful in implementing the changes. Your group members will not learn, will not have the information they need to make shifts, and will not feel they share in the change unless you involve them in the planning and implementation.

Sharing the "Big Picture"

People like to see the big picture of where the organization, department, or team is going. How does what is happening to them fit into the larger design for organizational change? People need to make sense of what is happening. They will experience less resistance and more energy as they are "pulled" toward a compelling vision of the future if they are able to see that the changes they are undergoing are making a difference in where the organization is going.

Set aside time to focus on the future with your team. Schedule a special meeting and ask your team to imagine themselves two to three years in the future, when the change has been completed successfully. Ask them to identify specific characteristics, behaviors, and results that they will experience. What is the organization like? What are people doing? What are work areas like? What type of work is being done? What improvements do they notice?

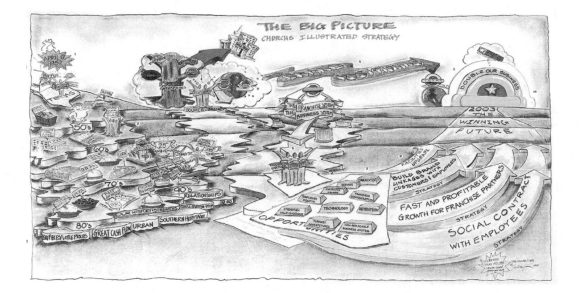

A Strategic Illustration of the vision provides a foundation for employees to discuss the stages of the journey. It allows employees to put various steps in perspective and not feel lost along the way.

Focus on What You Can Control

Most of the major organizational changes you will experience in your career will not be initiated by you. You may be able to anticipate change or see it coming (for example, the need for new technology, market focus, etc.), but most of the time you will be handed change as a fact. When this happens, a common reaction, regardless of level, is helplessness. "What can I do?" or "Has anyone taken us into account?" can lead to inactivity and frustration. Then workers spend their time bemoaning the change, dreaming of the old days, or criticizing the judgment of top management.

Your task as change agent is to shift the energy away from feelings of powerlessness toward seeing the opportunities of the future. You can do this by calling attention to the ways your team can make a difference.

Preparing for Change

Using the worksheet on the following page will help you prepare your thoughts to lead your team through the change-planning steps. You will learn that your team will see things differently from you, just as you often see things differently from your organizational leaders.

For now, though, think about a recent change in your organization, and describe in the worksheet's first column which aspects of the change are givens. Usually these are beyond your control. They could include aspects of timing, personnel, budget, or other factors.

Next, fill in the "Controllable" column with those aspects of the change that you and your team can *control*. This is where you need to dig. Some things may seem to be givens but may be within your control. These could include pace, resource allocation, or involvement of key stakeholders.

Finally, think about what aspects of the change you and your team can *negotiate*. Remember, you can always communicate or negotiate with other groups in your organization. Your group can initiate communication and discussion with any other group. What aspects of the change do you need to talk about, to have clarified, or to present new information about? How can you accomplish this?

Taking control and exerting influence are crucial aspects of change management. By the end of this book, you will regard almost everything about a change as negotiable. Top management does not automatically consider everything. If your team has better information or sees things differently, you owe it to your organization to negotiate and discuss it.

PREPARING FOR CHANGE WORKSHEET

Think about a recent change in your organization and, in the spaces provided, describe which aspects of that change were givens, which were negotiables, and which were controllable:

Givens	Negotiables	Controllable
Aspects of the Change We Cannot Control, Do Not Have Direct Choice Over	Aspects of the Change We Can Influence or Discuss with Other Groups	Aspects of the Change My Team Can Control

Five Phases in Planning for Change

Introducing and implementing a change in your group generally involves five key phases. You and your team will need to do your homework to complete each one. The five phases are:

Phase 1: *Aligning*
Phase 2: *Planning*
Phase 3: *Designing*
Phase 4: *Implementing*
Phase 5: *Rewarding*

Depending on circumstances, you may not go through the phases in order, but at least you should be aware of them. Otherwise you risk being inadequately prepared for implementing change successfully. Let's look at each phase in step-by-step detail.

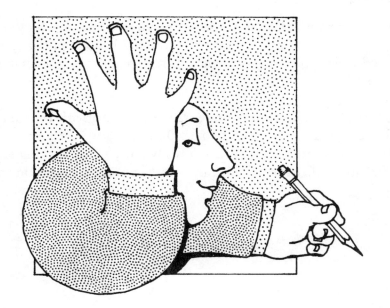

Phase 1: Aligning

Aligning means identifying the purpose for the change and a vision of what it will be like when it is completed successfully. Anticipate key elements and identify key linkages with other groups in the following ways:

1. **Prepare your employees.** Help employees understand how this change is linked to the overall organizational strategy and market conditions. Let them know what is happening ahead of time. Telling them too far ahead of time is not always better.

2. **Describe the change as completely as you can.** Emphasize your vision of how things will be when the change is successfully completed. Ask employees how they see the change affecting them individually and the work group as a whole? Identify who will be most affected and approach them first.

3. **Research what happened during the last change.** Does your group have a positive history of their ability to manage change, or was the last change traumatic? Learn from experience and let this background influence your current actions. Incorporate learnings; do not make the same mistakes twice.

4. **Assess the organizational readiness of your team.** Are they ready to undertake a change? An organization or group that is not mentally and emotionally prepared will tend to stay in denial, rather than accept the change and move on.

5. **Do not make additional changes that aren't critical.** People need all the stability they can get during change. Do not change the payroll dates, the working hours, or cafeteria procedures when you are making large-scale organizational changes. Change the most important things one at a time.

Phase 2: Planning

Planning requires getting people together to understand the environment in which the change is taking place and to map out strategy and implementation. Think it through by following these steps:

1. **Make contingency plans.** Think of options to the proposed change. If things go one way, what will you do? What about the other way? Anticipate the unforeseen, the unexpected, and any setbacks.

2. **Allow for the impact of change on personal performance and productivity.** Do not expect people to get up to speed in an instant. It will frustrate whatever sense of achievement they are experiencing. Predict "bumps in the road."

3. **Encourage employee input.** Discuss at each phase of the process and ask for suggestions. What did they see that you did not? Encourage their ideas.

4. **Anticipate the skills and knowledge that will be needed to master the change.** Look at the gap in the skills that people will need to successfully adapt to the change. Do your people have them? Have you prepared training plans?

5. **Clarify how you will measure success.** Set a timetable and objectives so you can measure your progress. Meet and assess your progress. Adjust thinking and focus as needed.

Phase 3: Designing

Designing involves defining the new structures, roles, decision making, and leadership, in the following ways:

1. **Create a transition management team to oversee the change.** This group is responsible for coordinating and integrating multiple efforts. Take the pulse of the organization and help identify possible roadblocks. Meet frequently to monitor the unforeseen, to give feedback, or to check on what is happening. Make feedback a daily event.

2. **Develop new policies and procedure.** Demonstrate flexibility to try new things. Loosen control and procedures. Encourage self-management. Allow innovation.

3. **Create new communication channels.** Remind people why the change makes sense. Use Web sites, intranets, collaborative forums, "big picture" maps, all-hands meetings, and training sessions so people will receive information fast. The cost of gossip is high; prevent it through clear, accurate communication.

4. **Create new organizational structures that will support the new focus.** Reconfigure leadership and management to attend to the performance of the new structure.

Phase 4: Implementing

Implementing means going live with the change—learning, and adjusting. Take clear, flexible action to accomplish these goals:

1. **Set up pilots;** try things out.

2. **Encourage self-management.** Inform all individuals that they are accountable for some aspect of the change. Clarify expectations and roles.

3. **Give more feedback** than usual to ensure that people always know where they stand.

4. **Allow for resistance.** Help people let go of the "old." Prepare to help those having special difficulty making the adjustment.

5. **Give people a chance to step back and take a look at what is going on.** Keep asking, "Is the change working the way we want it to?"

6. **Encourage people to think and act creatively.**

7. **Provide appropriate training** in new skills and coaching in new values and behaviors.

8. **Collaborate.** Build bridges from your work group to other work groups. Look for opportunities to interface your activities.

9. **Monitor the change process.** Conduct surveys to find out how employees are responding to the change.

Phase 5: Rewarding

Rewarding involves acknowledging the people who made it work. Share the gains and capture the learning in the following ways:

1. **Create incentives for special effort.** Celebrate those who lead the change. Give one-time bonuses to groups that come through the change smoothly.

2. **Celebrate by creating public displays** to acknowledge groups and individuals that help make things happen.

3. **Capture the learning and gathering experiences and share with other parts of the organization.**

4. **Build best practices** from your experience and other organizations'.

5. **Network** with other organizations at professional conferences.

6. **Acknowledge your results in organizational forums,** such as meetings, Web sites, and intranets.

Fantasies About Change

Managers tend to believe that change can be instant, painless, and quick—that the changes they make will:

➤ Not be disruptive

➤ Cost little and be quick to implement

➤ Solve previous organizational problems

But organizations are interconnected systems, so changing one thing often leads to unintended consequences in some other part of the organization. The best approach is to predict that the change will be challenging and not gloss over people's concerns. The more planning and involvement of those directly affected by the change, the sooner the new level of organizational capability can be reached. These topics are the focus of the next two parts of this book.

Understanding Change

> " *Things fall apart. The center will not hold.*"

—W.B. Yeats

Recognizing That Change Involves Loss

Change occurs when something ends and something new or different starts. Usually it means moving from the familiar to the unknown. The period between these two points is transition, in which people have to learn to let go of the old and embrace the new. Thus, change always involves loss.

It is important to understand that people are not weak or old-fashioned if they experience loss caused by change. This is a normal part of transition. In fact, people who do not display any feeling of loss often save it up and become overwhelmed by a seemingly small transition. It is healthier for all those involved to express and acknowledge loss when it occurs so they can move through the transition more quickly.

Even when change is positive—promotion, expansion, going public, new markets—it is not uncommon for people to feel an ending, or loss, associated with it. This is because change may make them feel:

➤ Their security is threatened

➤ Their sense of competence is threatened

➤ They may fail at the new tasks

➤ They are comfortable with the status quo

Even when the change is positive, patterns of success are disrupted and relationships have to change. It can be a struggle to accept a new direction. Managers often have a hard time understanding the loss associated with this kind of change. They do not realize how upsetting it is to give up familiar work patterns, even for something positive.

Acknowledging Loss to Manage Change

Many managers think that if they just tell their employees to "change," they will. But one job of a manager is to acknowledge that a loss has occurred, not pretend it is business as usual. Managers must always remember how much will be disrupted and understand that people need time to adjust. Unacknowledged loss will usually lead to resistance and disruption down the road.

The most common error in managing any kind of change is underestimating the effect it has on people. Change may manifest in a wide range of physical symptoms (such as headaches, body aches, sleep loss, or emotional distress), all of which will affect the quality of work. If you do not manage loss, you cannot lead people successfully in a new direction.

Common Losses from Workplace Change

Any type of loss, even of a work space or familiar technology, can trigger an emotional response that resembles grief. You must help your employees move past their loss, to accept and move forward in the new direction. Employees normally experience feelings of loss in several areas:

➤ **Security**–Employees no longer feel in control or no longer know what the future holds or where they stand in the organization.

➤ **Competence**–Workers no longer feel they know what to do or how to manage. People sometimes become embarrassed when they are faced with new tasks or challenges. It is hard to admit you do not know how to do something, especially after earlier success.

➤ **Relationships**–The familiar contact with people such as old customers, co-workers, or managers can disappear. People often lose their sense of belonging to a team, a group, or the organization.

➤ **Sense of direction**–Employees lose an understanding of where they are going and why they are going there. Meaning and mission often become unclear.

➤ **Territory**–There is an uncertain feeling about the area that used to belong to them. This could be work space or job assignments. Territory includes psychological space as well as physical space.

➤ **Identity**–Change affects how people see themselves in the world. They identify with their team, product, or company and find it hard to know "who" they are when these structures change. When this changes, they need to re-set their identity.

Building Supportive Relationships to Ease Change

A common fantasy is that if you order people to change, they will. This belief often leads managers to behave like drill sergeants—ordering employees around. Usually the response to this approach will be resistance, defensiveness, or withdrawal.

People do not normally change their behavior simply from information. For example, how many people have quit smoking because of the written warning on the cigarette package?

It is far more common for people to change because of the support, encouragement, caring confrontation, and empathy of a *relationship*. Becoming a change leader by building supportive relationships is often a new skill for managers. The more involved you are with your team, and the more involved they are with each other, the easier change will be. Creating trusting relationships requires skill and can require managers to be more vulnerable and open to their team members. But managers who can create supportive relationships are more successful during periods of change because their teams will trust and follow them.

Incentives and Rewards

It is important to create incentives for those who adapt to change professionally and thoroughly. To become a change leader you might:

➤ Create public recognition opportunities to celebrate steps forward

➤ Reward those who remove roadblocks to change

➤ Give a one-time bonus or special acknowledgement to those acquiring the new skills and behaviors that make the change work

➤ Incorporate good ideas and new suggestions from team members as a regular part of your meetings

Transitioning Through Change

Change often involves elements of both danger and opportunity. When people approach a change, their first response might be to see it as a threat or a danger. When this happens, they fear and resist the change. Once the change occurs, however, it is not uncommon for those affected to begin getting used to it.

During the transition period, people begin to see that the change may lead to new opportunities. Some see that the new way may indeed be more effective and offer the potential for new freedom and power. Once people accept that a change can provide new opportunities and possibilities, the change is well on the way to successful implementation.

Think of a recent change you experienced:

_____

Write your reactions to this change in the spaces provided.

How did you experience this change in the beginning—as a danger or an opportunity?

_____

_____

How did you react when the actual change began to affect you directly?

_____

_____

How did you know that you were beginning to get "used to" the change?

_____

_____

What hidden opportunities or possibilities did you find in the change?

_____

_____

The Four Phases of Transition

These questions focus on the four major phases of transition: Denial, Resistance, Exploration, and Commitment. During change, people focus on the past and *deny* the change. Next people go through a period of preoccupation, wondering where they stand and how they will be affected. This is normally where *resistance* occurs. As they enter the *exploration* and *commitment* phases, they start to look toward the future and the opportunities it can bring. Most people move through these four phases in every transition. But individuals may proceed quickly or get bogged down in different phases. Effective leadership can help a group and each of its members individually move through the phases from denial to commitment.

➤ The denial phase reflects the ability to not focus on the changes' immediate impacts, often enabling people to continue to work hard and stay focused.

➤ After a while the impact of the change begins to disrupt the way things have been and disturb familiar ways of doing things, resulting in an experience of loss of control or certainty. People naturally resist feelings of loss with anger and blaming others.

➤ When the loss is acknowledged it makes it easier to begin to explore what to do with what is left. This phase represents experimentation, innovation, and discovery.

➤ Commitment is reached when the change has been integrated and a sense of comfort and completion is experienced. This forms the foundation for beginning the next change.

The Transition Curve^{SM}

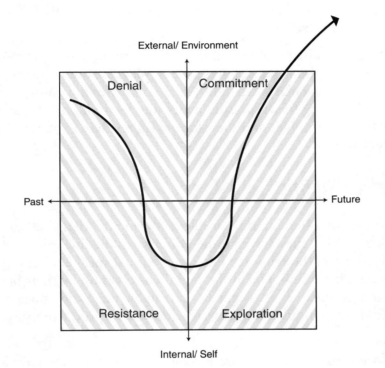

The sections that follow explain each of these phases in more detail.

---

*The Transition Curve^{SM} is a core tool of the Change Mastery and Change Leadership Training Programs and is used with permission from Changeworks Global, 461 Second Street #232, San Francisco, CA 94107, cscott@changeworksglobal.com.

The First Reaction to Change: Denial

When a big change is announced, often the first response is to go on as if nothing has happened. The announcement does not seem to sink in. Nothing happens. People continue to work as usual. It appears that productivity will continue and nothing will be affected.

The *denial* stage can be prolonged if employees are not encouraged to express their concerns or if management acts as if employees should just move directly into the new ways. Denial is harmful when it impedes the natural progression of letting go and moving forward. Employees stay focused on the way things were, neglecting both themselves and their future, rather than exploring how they can or need to change.

The Tarzan Swing^{SM}

Because people are often blind to problems during the denial phase, managers can mistakenly think they have jumped directly to the final phase of commitment. This hope can be reinforced by motivational speakers who simplistically encourage people to think positively, pull themselves up by their bootstraps, and move on to excellence. This is called a Tarzan Swing^{SM} and appears to work for a short while—usually until some indicator shows that productivity is decreasing.

At this point, an organization often calls on a consultant to "fix" problems, such as "stress" that employees are experiencing. The focus on the individual, rather than on the organization's response to the change, leaves an important side of change management untouched.

Top management is particularly prone to want their organizations to perform the Tarzan Swing^{SM} after the initial change announcement. These managers often do not see why people should have trouble. They seem to believe that people are being paid to put aside their feelings, or they may feel that the company simply does not have time to move through the other stages. But wishing does not change the sequence; it just drives it underground.

The Second Phase: Resistance

Resistance is not only a predictable part of change, but also perhaps the most difficult phase to deal with. It occurs when people have moved through the numbness of denial and begin to experience self-doubt, anger, anxiety, frustration, or uncertainty because of the change.

Some organizational changes can be compared to grief related to the death of a loved one. If a company is sold or merged, or if there are layoffs, people commonly experience the loss of expectations, hopes, promises, and work relationships.

In the resistance phase, productivity dips drastically and people are often upset and negative. Managers hear lots of grumbling, the personnel department is extra busy, and the copy machines churn out resumes. Accidents, sickness, and work-related absences multiply. Organizational resistance also can lead to lowered productivity and even sabotage. Outside programs on change management are most often requested during the resistance phase.

Allowing Employees to Express Resistance

Compared to enduring complaints or suffering blame from team members, denial looks much easier to many managers. Sometimes managers even encourage their team members to remain in the denial phase because it is an easier phase for them to manage. But resistance is a good sign—a sign that your group has left the state of denial and is ready to move through change. Even though the resistance may be misdirected at first, it shows that a person's system of self-defense is beginning to kick in; this is an important step in recovering from change.

Allowing people to express their feelings and share their experiences makes this phase pass faster. People who believe they are the only ones who feel a certain way, or think their reactions are more intense than their colleagues', feel better when they learn through sharing that others feel the same.

Your job as a manager is to stay in relationship with your employees as they express "blame, discomfort, exasperation, etc." with the change. This can often lead to them focusing on you personally—understand that your role is to acknowledge their experience but not feel guilty that you can't fix it.

Eventually everyone reaches a low point and begins to move up the other side of the change curve. This shift, clearly felt but different for everyone, indicates things are getting better. Work groups suddenly notice a renewed interest in work and feel creativity coming back. This signals that the resistance phase is passing.

How Much Resistance Should I Expect?

The amount of resistance is related to the depth of the disruption of the change. This differs with individuals and teams, explaining why different groups experience the same change differently.

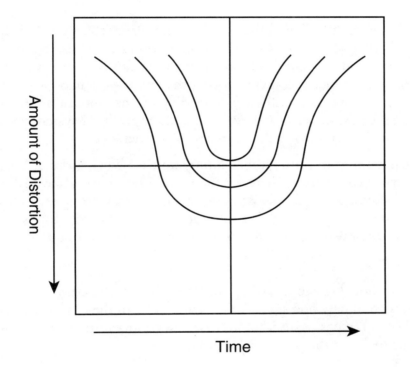

Using Ritual to Transition Out of Resistance

Not providing a forum in which people can express their betrayal and disappointment will prolong the resistance phase. During the resistance period, organizations can make effective use of organizational rituals (e.g., picnics, parties, awards, luncheons, etc.) to provide an opportunity for employees to express their appreciation of the past, acknowledgement that things have changed, and hope for the future.

One of the most successful things a manager can do during change is to help employees say "good good-byes"—so they can say "good hellos" during the exploration and commitment phases. A key element of this process involves accepting the discouragement, sadness, or grief that employees may be feeling. The strength of these emotions will vary depending on the amount of loss they are experiencing. For example, "good-bye" to an old procedural system will be much less emotional than moving the business to another state.

One way to help employees through this bumpy time is by using ritual. We are not suggesting tribal ceremonies; there are plenty of modern rituals available. The most successful ones are simple ways to publicly acknowledge losses. Any gathering that brings everyone together to remember the past, tell stories about it, and acknowledge how important it was at the time serves as an effective ritual. For example:

> ➤ A public housing agency, when moving from an old, crumbling building to a new one across town, cut a piece of the old carpet (the symbol of the past), put it up in their new lounge, and covered it with mementos from the previous location.

> ➤ During a merger, employees assembled a time capsule and buried it with old memos, reports, and so on. As they threw dirt on it, they told stories about the past.

Events like these have a way of springing up spontaneously. Management often makes the mistake of thinking such events are childish or unnecessary. But when people are not given an opportunity to grieve, they move forward at a slower pace. In the long run, this holds up productivity and prolongs resistance.

Saying good-bye is especially important for people left behind in a reorganization, merger, or buyout. The "survivors" often feel guilty, bitter, distrustful, and depressed. Those left behind need a chance to say good-bye to the people who have gone.

Other ways to focus these sessions is to identify:

➤ What is important to "keep" from the old way

➤ What needs to be "dropped" or released

➤ What needs to be "created" to move forward

Think of a change you are going through. What kind of event could you initiate to help your people say good-bye in a positive way?

_____

_____

_____

_____

The Final Phases: Exploration and Commitment

During the *exploration* phase, energy is released as people focus their attention on the future and toward the external environment once again. People are somewhat chaotic as they try to figure out new responsibilities, search for new ways to relate to each other, learn more about their future, and wonder how the new organization will work. There is uncertainty during this phase, including stress among those who need a lot of structure. During exploration, people tend to draw on their internal creative energy to figure out ways to capitalize on the future. This phase can be exciting and exhilarating. It can create powerful new bonds in a work group.

Committing to a New Way of Working

After searching, testing, experimenting, and exploring, a new pattern of working begins to emerge. When this happens, the individual or group is ready for *commitment*. During this phase employees are ready to focus on a plan. They are willing to re-create their mission and build action plans to make it work. They are prepared to learn new ways to work together and have renegotiated roles and expectations.

The values and actions needed to commit to a new phase of productivity are in place. This is the phase during which employees are willing to solidly identify with a set of goals and be clear about how to reach them. This phase will last until a new cycle of transition begins with another major change.

Because change is inevitable, a good question might be: Will we always be riding on this wave of transition? The ideal answer is yes, for without change, we and our organizations would become stale and unresponsive.

The challenge is learning to move through the transition as easily and creatively as possible. What helps people navigate through unknown territory is a map of what they can expect—provided by the Transition Curve[SM]—and information on ways to respond most effectively to the predictable challenges that are presented.

Identifying the Phases in Your Team's Behavior

At any point during the change process, your team will probably not be in just one phase, but shifting back and forth between phases. As a change leader, you must be able to identify which phase your general group is in as well as the phase each individual is experiencing. This way, you can respond with the right management strategy to help your team move through the Transition Curve^{SM} toward commitment.

Transition Curve^{SM} Behaviors

The example behaviors listed below for each phase will help you identify where team members stand so you can provide the most helpful response. Remember people are often experiencing multiple changes and are often in multiple phases—don't pigeonhole people.

➤ **Denial:** It is common to observe withdrawal, "business as usual," and a focus on the past. There is activity, but not much gets done.

➤ **Resistance:** You will see anger, blame, anxiety, and even "retirement" on the job. "What's the difference? This company doesn't care anymore."

➤ **Exploration:** You will recognize over-preparation, confusion, chaos, energy—lots of energy and new ideas but a lack of focus. "Let's try this and this and what about this...."

➤ **Commitment:** Employees begin working together. There is cooperation and a better focus. "How can we work on this?" Those who are committed are looking for the next challenge.

Change Diagnostic Tool

It is often helpful to think about where your team is in the change process. This will help you adjust your leadership/management strategy for maximum effectiveness. Another way to identify which stage employees are in is with the Change Diagnostic Tool that follows. Check any behaviors that you observed to suggest what phase of change is taking place.

Denial

❑ *"It will be over real soon"*
❑ Apathy/inattention
❑ Numbness
❑ Hard at work

Commitment

❑ Cooperation
❑ Satisfaction
❑ Clear focus and plan
❑ Focus on work

Resistance

❑ Edginess
❑ Anger/disagreements
❑ Feeling betrayed
❑ Withdrawal from the team
❑ Worry

Exploration

❑ Overpreparation
❑ Frustration
❑ Too many new ideas
❑ Have too much to do
❑ Cannot focus

Management Strategies for Each Phase

As you have seen, each transition phase is expressed with different behaviors. Your approach will need to match the phase people are experiencing. And it is not uncommon to find an employee swinging between two stages. When this happens, use the strategy suggested for the earlier stage until that person is ready to move forward.

➤ **During Denial**

Confront individuals with information. Let them know that the change will happen. Explain what to expect and suggest actions they can take to adjust to the change. Give them time to let things sink in, and then schedule a planning session to talk things over.

➤ **During Resistance**

Listen, acknowledge feelings, respond empathetically, and provide support. Do not try to talk people out of their feelings or tell them to "change" or pull together. If you accept their response, they will continue to tell you how they are feeling. This will help you respond to some of their concerns.

➤ **During Exploration**

Focus on priorities and provide any needed training. Follow up on projects underway. Set short-term goals. Conduct brainstorming and planning sessions.

➤ **During Commitment**

Talk about long-term vision. Set long-term goals. Concentrate on team building. Create a mission statement. Validate and reward those responding to the change. Look ahead and focus on the next changes anticipated.

The Troubled Employee

Organizational change is hard enough. When it happens along with other personal problems, it may feel like "the straw that broke the camel's back." It is estimated that 10–15% of the employee population at any given time have alcohol or drug or other medical or behavioral problems that prevent them from being fully productive. The added stress of change on individuals who are barely coping can be devastating.

All the management strategies in the world will not help them. They need professional assistance. Because personal problems increase during periods of stress, such as change, you will probably see an increase in troubled behavior during these times. The safest path is to refer any employee needing attention to professional help through your employee medical or Employee Assistance Program (EAP). Contact your personnel or human resources department for more information.

Remember, covering up poor performance simply extends the time the employee will be distressed before getting help. Avoiding a problem is a form of denial.

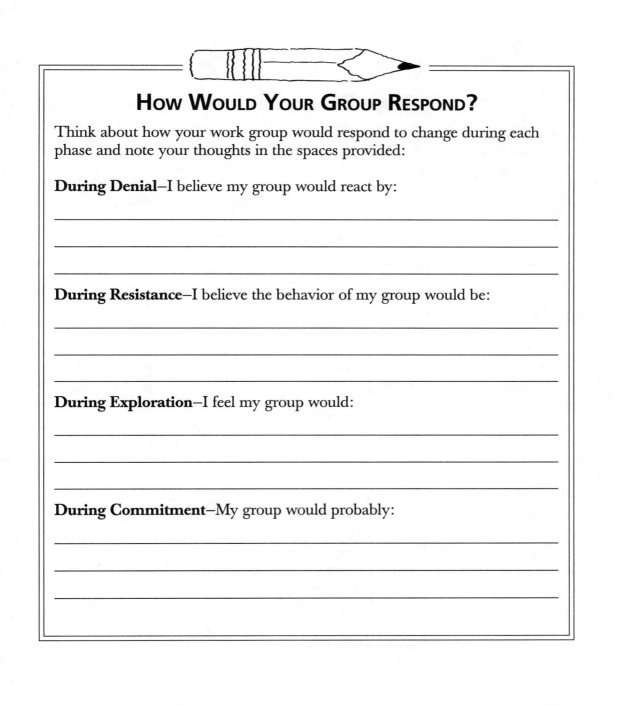

HOW WOULD YOUR GROUP RESPOND?

Think about how your work group would respond to change during each phase and note your thoughts in the spaces provided:

During Denial—I believe my group would react by:

_____

_____

_____

During Resistance—I believe the behavior of my group would be:

_____

_____

_____

During Exploration—I feel my group would:

_____

_____

_____

During Commitment—My group would probably:

_____

_____

_____

TEAM DIAGNOSTIC TOOL

To help you plan, use the Team Diagnostic Tool to find out what strategy to start with. List a few key people in your group and, based on the indicators mentioned on the previous pages, identify which phase each member is in.

	Name	**Signs Observed**	**Phase**
1.	_____	_____	_____
2.	_____	_____	_____
3.	_____	_____	_____
4.	_____	_____	_____
5.	_____	_____	_____

Next, graph your members on the change grid below. Place their initials about where they fall on the curve.

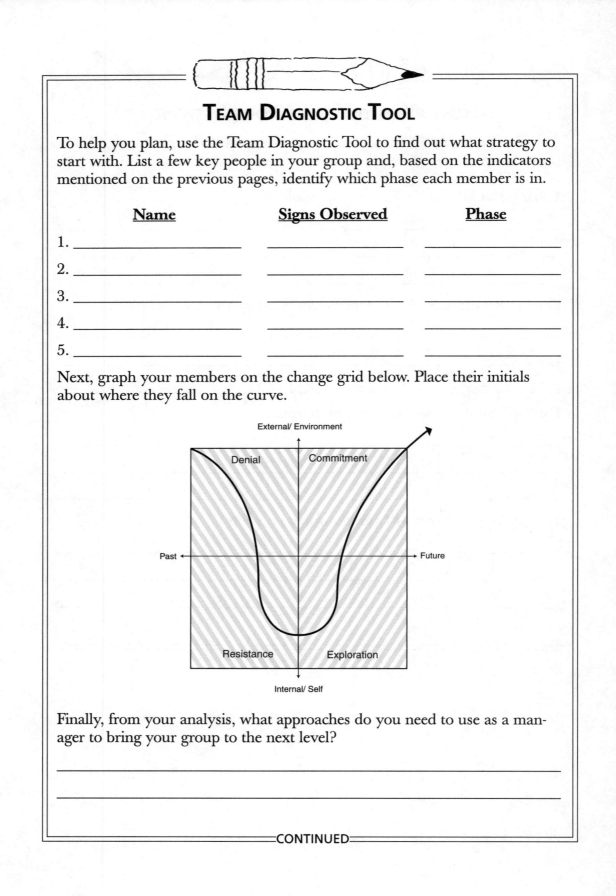

Finally, from your analysis, what approaches do you need to use as a manager to bring your group to the next level?

_____

_____

CONTINUED

CONTINUED

Who are the leaders that can help others move along?

_____

_____

Who are the people in your group who might need special help?

_____

_____

Beware the Traps of Transitioning Too Quickly

As you have learned, people may go through the four phases of transition at different rates, but they generally do need to go through all four phases. Failing to realize this and pushing people through phases before they are ready can lead managers to fall into one of the following traps:

➤ **Ignoring or resisting resistance**

Resistance is not pleasant to experience. It can feel like everyone is angry with you and you are to blame. This is normally temporary. Denying resistance only makes it go deeper and last longer. Invite it. Seek it out through listening and good questioning.

➤ **Jumping to team building**

When faced with change, many managers think that what they need most is getting people back to working together. When a group is in denial, resistance, or the early moments of exploration, you are wasting time working on team building. The group needs a chance to complain and assess their loss before beginning to rebuild trust and cooperation.

➤ **The "Drano" approach—pushing productivity too soon**

Some managers believe that if you demand performance you will get it. Employees may respond in the short run but then tend to plateau and actually decrease productivity if their feelings do not match their actions. The danger is that you will end up with a "clogged" organization where everything breaks down.

Eight Guidelines for Leading Change

Whether you and your team are transitioning into a new organization, a new task, or a new technology, all of you will need to learn how to work together differently. As the leader, you will need to understand how relationships within your unit will change along with what you expect from one another and how you will work together.

Armed with a fuller understanding of how change affects people and how to manage your team through the transition, which you have learned in Part 2, you are ready to learn how to lead your team effectively in implementing workplace and organizational changes. The following guidelines are a preview of what is to come in Part 3—Leading Change:

1. **Have a good reason for making the change.** Changes are usually made for a good reason. Take them seriously. Make sure you understand why you are making the change and how it ties to the larger organizational strategy.

2. **Involve people in the change.** People who are involved are less likely to resist. Being a part of the planning gives people a sense of control. Ask for opinions about how they would do it. Consider conducting surveys, town hall meetings, focus groups, and polls.

3. **Put a respected person in charge.** Each change needs a leader. Select someone who is seen in a positive light by the group.

4. **Create transition management teams.** You need a dedicated, representative cross-section team from your group to plan, anticipate, troubleshoot, coordinate, and focus the change efforts. You cannot do it alone.

5. **Provide opportunities to see the "big picture."** People need to see how they fit in and the skills to understand how to succeed in the new way. Bring groups together to have conversations about what this means and build new skills.

6. **Use outside catalysts.** For some reason, there is often more power in what an outsider says than in the same suggestions coming from inside. Partner with outsiders to reinforce the direction in which you want to go. Outsiders bring important information and a fresh perspective.

7. **Establish symbols of change.** Encourage the development of newsletters, new logos or slogans, and recognition events to help celebrate and reflect the change.

8. **Acknowledge and reward people.** As change begins to work, take time to recognize and recall the achievements of the people who made it happen. Acknowledge the struggle and sacrifices people have made.

Leading Change

"
I must follow the people. Am I not their leader?"

—Benjamin Disraeli

Communicating About Change

As a manager in a time of change, you are often caught in the middle. You may have a lot, some, or almost no input in the change, yet you have a responsibility to make it work in your unit. You have your own feelings to consider. The sooner you move through your own denial and resistance the sooner you'll be able to lead others.

The way you bring the message about a change to your team has much to do with the eventual outcome. How you make your announcement, what you say, and how you negotiate with your team members will make the difference. This part provides guidance for announcing change, tells how to monitor responses, and covers negotiating for what needs to be done.

The change announcement is most often made during the denial phase of the transition and sometimes does not sink in. When the message is accepted, your group may shift from denial to resistance very quickly. You need to learn how to manage these intense responses from your team.

Setting a Climate for Communication

In times of change, maintaining open communication can help prevent rumors, anxiety, and mistakes. Often managers avoid delivering unsettling news by claiming they are "too busy and pressured" to take time to meet with their people. Studies have shown that if you do not make time early in the process, you will spend more time later cleaning up the problems.

During change, two-way communication is essential. Every issue must be covered. Different communication forms are recommended. Use open forums, newsletters, videos, Web sites/Intranets, fireside chats, informal discussions—whatever works for you. Repeat the message using various methods of communication regularly.

Guidelines for Informing Your Team

People who go most successfully through change benefit from:

➤ Specific reasons for the change

➤ Accurate information

➤ An opportunity to ask questions

➤ An opportunity to express their feelings

➤ Personal reassurance

With this in mind, using the following tips will help you inform your team about change. Place a check mark (✔) beside those you currently use. Place an "X" next to those you intend to use during the next change.

❑ **Explain the reasons for the change**

Tell people clearly "why" the change is necessary and give them as much data as possible. Keep them informed of any new developments. Tie the change to larger organizational success.

❑ **Talk to people in person**

A memo, newsletter, voice mail, or e-mail is not the most effective way to inform people about important changes. Written announcements do not allow people to express their feelings directly. Written documents are often used to avoid dealing with people's responses. In the long run, this can only backfire. Voice mails and e-mails are good as a follow-up after a one-on-one meeting because people can be in denial and have a hard time hearing information that disturbs their security.

❑ **Tell people the truth**

The more informed people are, the less anxious they will be. Unanswered questions are fuel for the rumor mill. If you do not know, tell them so. You do not have to know all the answers. A believable leader does not know everything, especially in times of change. Solicit questions and try to find answers to the missing information. Schedule another meeting when you learn more and share that information as it becomes available.

❏ **Express your feelings**

Do not exclude information about your feelings. People want to know your reactions. They will feel acknowledged and understood and will be more open if your feelings are expressed. When appropriate, tell them how the change affects you personally. Self-disclosure from a leader is a very powerful strategy because you often reflect what they are thinking.

❏ **Take first steps**

Encourage people to immediately take a step toward the new direction or the new skill. The biggest obstacle to change just may be getting over the inertia of getting started.

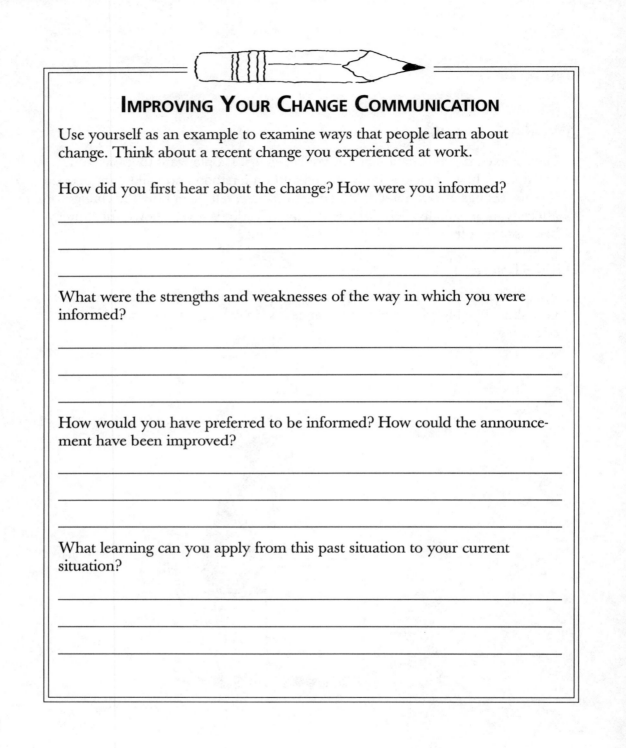

IMPROVING YOUR CHANGE COMMUNICATION

Use yourself as an example to examine ways that people learn about change. Think about a recent change you experienced at work.

How did you first hear about the change? How were you informed?

_____

_____

_____

What were the strengths and weaknesses of the way in which you were informed?

_____

_____

_____

How would you have preferred to be informed? How could the announcement have been improved?

_____

_____

_____

What learning can you apply from this past situation to your current situation?

_____

_____

_____

Meeting with Employees Throughout the Change Process

A meeting to announce a change is the best way to inform your group. Meetings with your employees also are basic tools for planning, implementing, and monitoring change. They reinforce the idea that people can work together to make things happen as a team. Meetings can let everyone know what is happening and offer opportunities for feedback.

During change, you should schedule frequent meetings, both formal and informal, to ensure that communication is clear and open. Keeping everyone informed is the overall objective even though the specific purpose of each meeting will vary as you move through the stages of the change process. The following are some specific purposes for meetings:

➤ To announce a change

➤ To provide new information and clarification

➤ To give people a supportive place to express their feelings

➤ To involve employees in the planning and implementation of the change

➤ To provide feedback on how things are going

➤ Other purposes: _____

_____

_____

Generally, it is best to meet with your whole group if the change affects all of them. If some people are more directly affected, you might meet with them individually immediately before the group meeting so you can explain the situation carefully and offer support if appropriate. If individuals will be negatively affected, a pre-meeting will give you the opportunity to deal with this.

CHANGE ANNOUNCEMENT WORKSHEET

When it is time to announce a change, prepare by filling out this worksheet before you hold the change meeting.

What is the change? (Be specific.)

_____

_____

What is the reason for the change? Why now?

_____

_____

Likely impact to the organization/to our group?

_____

_____

Benefits?

_____

_____

Drawbacks?

_____

_____

Details known?

_____

_____

Details not known?

_____

_____

Planning and Leading a Change Meeting

As with any important business activity, conducting a change meeting requires that you do your homework beforehand. Review the information to be communicated. Fill out the Change Announcement Worksheet and write notes to ensure that all key information is presented. Think about the best way to introduce the change and the most logical way to present the details.

Following is a general format for a change meeting. Engaging people in the change takes time. You will probably have a series of meetings to discuss the following topics:

➤ Review the need for change and how it came about

➤ Describe the change in detail

➤ Explain how the change will affect your group

➤ Ask for questions about the change; invite participation

➤ Listen to feelings and respond appropriately

➤ Share your personal feelings (if appropriate)

➤ Ask for help and support in making the change work

Four Transition Phases in One Meeting

Be aware that meetings in which change is announced sometimes reflect a miniature version of the four phases of the transition cycle. First, there can be *denial* until the announcement is discussed and understood. Then people may express *resistance* by questioning, complaining, or second-guessing. Next, there can be a shift toward *exploration* as people begin to question how they will respond to the future with some constructive brainstorming and planning. Finally, the group may tentatively *commit* to the direction of the change.

In these and all meetings about change, keep the lines of communication open by applying the following tips:

➤ Talk to people in person

➤ Tell people the truth

➤ Express your feelings

➤ Involve everyone in planning

➤ Tell people the history of the change

➤ Break the change into steps

➤ Take time; be patient

Formulating Your Message

During change, managers often assume that others will understand what to do. Because of increased pressure, there is sometimes a tendency to shorten directions or reduce communications. This is unfortunate because more information is needed during change, not less. The following is a four-part formula that will help you communicate clearly:

Behavior + Feelings + Effects + Needs = Clear Communication

Let's look at the parts in more detail:

1. Behavior/Situation:

What has happened? What is the change that needs to be responded to?

"Since we've started using the new application, absenteeism has increased significantly. Let's discuss the situation to see if we can discover the reasons."

2. Feelings:

What are your feelings about the change? Are you confused, hopeful, or upset?

"I'm a little frustrated about this outcome of the change and want to learn more about what you think is involved."

3. Effects:

What effect will the change have on you? The work group? The project?

"The effect of the change has been to put us behind schedule for April."

4. Needs/Wants:

What outcome would you like to see? What do you want the other person to do?

"What I'd like is to see if we can figure out what is happening and what we can do to get back on track."

Choosing the Best Words to Communicate Feelings

Feelings are the hardest to communicate because many people have a harder time putting words to their experience. And people from different cultural backgrounds and age groups may hear words differently.*

Verbalizing your feelings can cause your listener to withdraw or become defensive. But that does not have to happen. One of the ways to reduce the likelihood of this reaction is to select the least intense words to describe your feelings. This gives the listener most opportunity for having a dialogue to understand the source of the concern. Choosing appropriate words can help. It is usually best to select the least dramatic words that still communicate how you feel.

Think of feeling words as belonging to three different categories:

➤ **MILD** conveys minimal amount of emotional impact. Examples: confused, curious, concerned, interested. These are the most likely to encourage dialogue and problem-solving conversation.

➤ **MEDIUM** Examples: distressed, upset, frustrated.

➤ **STRONG** are very strong. Examples: appalled, aghast, betrayed, deceived.

*For an excellent book on this subject, read *Working Together,* by George Simons, Crisp Publications.

SENDING A CLEAR MESSAGE

Think of the change you are facing. Is there one person you need to inform about a particular response or difficulty you are having? What message(s) do you need to deliver? Use the formula as outlined below to write your message.

1. **Behavior/Situation that is occuring...**

_____

_____

_____

2. **Feelings I am having...**

_____

_____

_____

3. **Effects on my performance...**

_____

_____

_____

4. **Need to move forward...**

_____

_____

_____

Better Communication Through Active Listening

Some managers frustrate their teams by spending the whole meeting talking. They are so busy announcing, explaining, and persuading that they do not leave time for feedback. Perhaps they fear hearing responses. The secret of being a successful change leader is not only talking openly and directly, but also listening carefully to what is said (and sometimes what is not said).

Listening will provide you with messages, meanings, and feelings that your team experiences. People who feel listened to are less resistant and often move through change more easily. Active listening is the best technique to help individuals understand their feelings and move more quickly to action.

Steps of Active Listening

When you engage in active listening, you not only pay attention to what people are saying but also to the feelings and underlying emotions that lie behind what they are saying. The goals of active listening are to help others express what they feel and want and to show that you understand their thinking. Follow these steps:

1. **Pay attention with your whole body.** Sit back and focus on the other person. Do not shuffle through papers or fidget. Focus on what the person says.

2. **Show interest.** Occasionally repeat what you heard the person say to verify the message. (e.g., *"Let's see, you're saying that the reorganization will disrupt your career plan."*)

3. **Ask open-ended questions.** Draw the person out. Often it takes time for people to express what they are trying to say. (e.g., *"What was your initial reaction to the change?"*)

4. **Listen to the feelings behind the message.** Hear more than just the content in what they are saying. You can check out what you are thinking by asking the person or group a question. (e.g., *"Are you all feeling a loss of your career plans?"*)

5. **Confirm and clarify what you have heard.** Make sure that you have understood what people are saying. Summarize the core of the message in a statement back to them. If you accurately confirm what they have been saying, they become more relaxed and receptive to further discussion. (e.g., *"What I understand now is that how most of you are really feeling is your career plans are disrupted by this change."*)

Responding to Indifference or Anger

Sometimes despite your best efforts at active listening, you are met only with anger responses—or no response at all. But rather than getting caught up in the other person's anger or shutting down communication altogether, you might try one or more of the following responses:

➤ **Postpone:** "You don't seem ready to talk, so perhaps we can meet later today."

➤ **Ask another open-ended question:** "What do you think of this change?"

➤ **Repeat:** "Now that I've explained the change, what do you think?"

➤ **Self-disclosure:** "The first time I heard about this I was very concerned. What about you?"

➤ **Other people's reactions:** "When the other department went through this change, their people were upset. How did you feel?"

➤ **Broken record:** Repeat what you have just said.

Setting the Stage for Engaging Your Team

People will more readily accept change if they participate in designing and planning it—if they have a role in defining how to meet a goal or respond to a new situation. Participation and collaboration can take many forms, including:

➤ Task forces

➤ Focus groups

➤ Opinion surveys

➤ All-hands meetings

➤ Collaborative forums

➤ Brainstorming meetings

As a manager, you want to use as many of these as you can to directly involve your employees in the change process. Increasing collaboration depends on the following steps:

➤ Creating a "safe zone" for free discussion

➤ Pressing for honest opinions

➤ Inviting differences of opinion

➤ Avoiding judging, criticizing, or blaming

➤ Sharing your dilemmas; asking for help from the team

Check Your Intentions

Before beginning to involve your employees in the change process, check your intention. Are you involving them because you honestly want to learn how they feel, or are you doing it simply to protect yourself from criticism? Many managers have tried involvement and failed because their intention was to protect themselves, not to learn.

Below are examples of assumptions that managers may be holding that lead them to pull back from involving employees.

❑ Employees need to be watched closely or they will take advantage of the company.

❑ Employees are incapable of suggesting the best way to get something done.

❑ Because of my experience I know how best to get the work done.

❑ I want my employees to come to me rather than solve problems by themselves.

If you checked any of the above boxes, you need to work on learning how to become a participatory manager who trusts employees enough to give them freedom to define their own ways of working.

Be aware, though, that despite the advantages of collaboration and participatory management, there are times, listed below, that group decisions and planning are not the best approach:

➤ When time is of the essence

➤ When one person has the expertise and a great track record

➤ When key people will not be affected

➤ When you cannot afford to make a mistake

Motivating Your Team to Get Involved

Motivating others has been thought of as something managers "do" to their employees. The implication is that managers are required to motivate others to change. But new thinking indicates that people do not have to be tricked or forced to work. In fact, studies show that most people want to do a good job.

Getting people motivated is not *making* people do things. It is uncovering the *"wanna"* factor, which is simply learning what they want to do. A majority of workers indicate they are not asked or expected to do all that they could in their job. They wish they could contribute even more!

Before, during, and after experiencing workplace change, specific conditions motivate employees. Make sure you provide as many of the following as possible:

➤ Work that is interesting and meaningful

➤ A clear statement of the results you expect

➤ Appropriate and on-time feedback on those results

➤ A reward system for achieving results

Promoting Collaboration

People get excited about change when they see a part for themselves in it. They respond with enthusiasm when they feel they have a role in helping define how their work group will be involved in the change. As interaction increases, so does the chance of a better decision. A good leader will offer opportunities for team members to be a part of making change work. This involves asking people for their ideas on how to do it best.

Getting Through Change Demands Collaboration

DIRECTIVE STYLE

Low Participation

Low Commitment

Leader is Responsible for Results

COLLABORATIVE STYLE

High Participation

High Commitment

Standard is Responsible for Results

Six Steps for Setting Goals Together

Even if the bigger direction of the change has been set, you can help your employees through change by ensuring you involve them in the setting of goals for their work. Participative goal setting requires open communication in a problem-solving environment.

Using the six-step process outlined as follows will guide you in involving your team in this give-and-take process. Remember that in times of change, goals and objectives can change frequently and should be reevaluated often.

Step 1: Assess the Current Situation

Does the new work after the change match the current objectives? How have expectations changed since they were last reviewed? Ask open-ended questions to find out how each employee feels about what is going on in relation to new work expectations. And let your employees tell you what is going on. Solicit their ideas on how best to accomplish new responsibilities by asking, "If you had to do this, how would you go about it?" or "If you were the boss and you wanted this to happen, how would you go about it?"

Step 2: Listen and Rephrase to Establish Trust

It is impossible to listen and talk at the same time. Listen for the main idea and take notes to ensure that you recall what the other person said. Allow enough time for employees to tell their own stories completely. Listen for emotion (what are they feeling at this time?). Encourage employees with affirmative head nods; occasionally say "uh huh," "go on," or "yes." Ask open-ended questions (using how, what, where, when, why) and then repeat or restate what you think the other person said. Ask a question to confirm your understanding.

Step 3: Clarify Objectives

Work together toward a clearer idea of what it is you want and need to achieve. Ask employees to write out their objectives. Then meet to discuss and revise them. Working together will motivate an employee to do well and will establish a focus for performance.

Remember, objectives are SMART:

S pecific about what is to be accomplished

M easurable

A ttainable

R esults or output-oriented

T ime bound

Step 4: Identify Problems

While setting goals, there will be some areas where you and your employees might not agree. During periods of change it is common to either have too many objectives (the result of combining jobs without cutting out objectives) or trying to do work that fits both the "old" and "new" way of doing things. As a manager, your job is to help rank objectives to prevent employees from becoming over-whelmed. Too many objectives create anxiety and lead to poor performance.

Step 5: Brainstorm Solutions

During change it is common for jobs to change focus and urgency and have different priorities. Previous job descriptions are often not accurate, and employees may feel upset if they are being asked to do things that are "not their job." To help employees understand their new roles, you need to think about:

What has been tried before?

_____

_____

What have other people done in similar situations?

_____

_____

What have you tried before that may not have worked then, but that might work now?

_____

_____

Step 6: Provide Feedback to Promote Motivation

Feedback is essential to employees during change. They need to know how they are doing. They need encouragement and support. Many managers do not do a good job of providing feedback when things are normal. When feedback is poor, employees are more likely to be anxious, have low job satisfaction, or quit. People who hear nothing usually fear the worst.

Check (✔) any of the following reasons you have used for not giving feedback and then vow to change your behavior:

❏ They already know what I think

❏ I'm the boss; they just need to follow my instructions

❏ I have too many other things to do

❏ If anything new happens, I'll tell those who need to know

❏ They're professionals—they shouldn't need their hands held

❏ _____

Maintaining Employee Involvement

As you have learned in the sections about transitioning through change, workplace changes will affect your employees' job performance. In the early stages of change, employees are often unmotivated, negative, or disinterested in the work that needs to be done. Their attention is elsewhere. They would not normally have a problem with motivation; but during workplace change, they are dealing with other issues besides the work at hand. Thus, the primary complaint of managers during workplace change is the difficulty they experience getting their people motivated.

Job performance usually will be affected in direct proportion to the magnitude of the change. If the change is significant, it is safe to assume that job activities will not be accomplished at a normal rate. Factor this slowdown in your production expectations and scheduling.

Managing Through Mistakes

Mistakes will be made during changes. How you respond to them will be important in maintaining employee involvement. Each mistake represents a potential for learning. It is your job to focus employees on the learning aspect of the mistake. Ask what they will do to prevent the mistake from happening again. Provide positive reinforcement to their ideas and give them your support to try again.

One way to reduce damage from mistakes is to have regular cycles of report and feedback. This is especially important during changes in which the previous ways of working are off the mark and need to be reconsidered.

Making the Work More Rewarding

During change you have an excellent opportunity to rethink job descriptions and assignments to make them more meaningful. Job enrichment can be nothing more than taking a current job and involving the employee to make it more meaningful. This may involve adding responsibilities, varying or rotating tasks, or getting the job done in new ways.

Describe a job in your work group that may be a candidate for enrichment.

_____

_____

_____

Becoming a Change Leader

Being a leader during change is not easy. Many managers say they feel powerless in their role during change, being squeezed between pressures from above and below. One thing you can do is set a vision for your own work group and re-affirm the values you will follow to achieve your results. As the span of your responsibility increases it's important to engage employees in understanding the broader meaning of their efforts. To bring this broader perspective:

➤ Articulate a vision of where the group is going

➤ Share that vision

➤ Create an environment where employees feel a sense of making the vision come true

Instead of waiting, empower your team to make the changes themselves with the following behaviors:

➤ **Focus on the process**–bring tough issues to the surface, pay attention to how things get done, manage context

➤ **Use a problem-solving orientation**–do not blame; fix systems, not people

➤ **Create a learning environment**–give lots of information and listen

➤ **Reward shared responsibility**–emphasize accountability and mutual contracts

Creating a Vision with Your Group

Working on a vision can be an exciting process. It can help employees realize they play a part in shaping their future. Rather than worrying about an uncertain future, visioning can help a team generate a shared sense of where they are headed. From the vision you create, it is possible to work backward to identify specific initiatives, goals, and actions that will lead toward the vision.

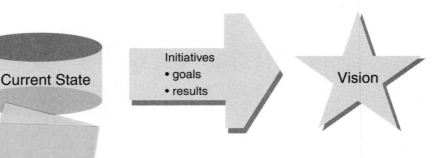

Current State

Initiatives
• goals
• results

Vision

How we get there...   Where we are going...

...ve have to move from "how it was" to a vision of "how it ...has progressed beyond denial and resistance, it is common ...n energy. People start preparing themselves to face the ...where they stand, new results that need to be achieved, and ...ahead.

...need help to create a vision, a "big picture" of where they ...u do not have all the answers, it is important to envision an ...e" of what success would look like.

...ues

Values are the foundation for the way you work together. During change, basic values may shift. For example, a company that once valued predictability may shift toward valuing innovation and new markets. Change can lead to a reconfiguration of the values by which your team operates. Clarify what the previous values have been and what the new values will be.*

---

* For more information on the process for doing team value clarification, read *Organizational Vision, Values, and Mission,* by Scott, Jaffe, and Tobe, Crisp Publications.

Creating a Change
Action Plan

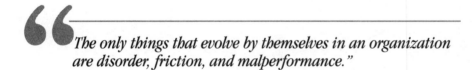

The only things that evolve by themselves in an organization are disorder, friction, and malperformance."

–Peter Drucker

An Action Plan for Success

Now it is time to put together all that you have learned and create an action plan for responding to change in your workplace. Take time to answer the questions below for changes you face:

1. Describe the change as completely as you can. State specifically how it will affect your employees, department, and organization. Note "human factors" that will be affected by the change.

_____

_____

2. What is your vision of the best possible outcome? What would success look like?

_____

_____

3. What are the strengths of your group or department in undertaking this change?

_____

_____

4. What are the obstacles that could prevent you from reaching your goal?

_____

_____

5. List your action steps for:

Communicating the change:

_____

_____

Dealing with resistance:

_____

_____

Involving the team:

_____

_____

Focusing leadership:

_____

_____

6. What is your timetable for making this change?

Start:_____

Finish:_____

7. What new skills, knowledge, and attitudes are needed to make this change?

Skills:

_____

_____

Knowledge:

_____

_____

Attitudes:

_____

_____

8. How will you acknowledge, recognize, and celebrate this change?

_____

_____

9. How will you create incentives to move toward change?

_____

_____

10. How will you reward yourselves for having led this change?

_____

_____

Recommended Reading

Deal, Terrence and William Kennedy. *Corporate Cultures*. Reading, MA: Addison-Wesley, 1982.

Galphin, Timothy J. *The Human Side of Change: A Practical Guide to Organization Redesign*. San Francisco: Jossey-Bass, 1996.

Jaffe, Dennis, Cynthia Scott, and Glenn Tobe. *Rekindling Commitment*. San Francisco: Jossey-Bass, 1994.

Jaffe, Dennis, and Cynthia Scott. *Getting Your Organization to Change*. San Francisco: Jossey-Bass Publishers, 1999.

Kanter, Rosabeth Moss. *Evolve: Succeeding in the Digital Culture of Tomorrow*. Boston: Harvard Business School Press, 2001.

Kanter, Rosabeth Moss. *The Change Masters*. NY: Simon and Schuster, 1983.

Morgan, Gareth. *Riding the Waves of Change*. San Francisco: Jossey-Bass, 1988.

Peters, Tom. *Thriving on Chaos*. NY: Alfred A. Knopf, 1988.

Scott, Cynthia and Dennis Jaffe. *Managing Personal Change*. Boston, MA: Thomson Learning/Course Technology, 1989.

Scott, Cynthia and Dennis Jaffe. *Take This Work and Love It*. Boston, MA: Thomson Learning/Course Technology, 1997.

Scott, Cynthia, Dennis Jaffe, and Glenn Tobe. *Organizational Vision, Values, and Mission*. Boston, MA: Thomson Learning/Course Technology, 1993.

Senge, Peter, Art Kleiner, Charlotte Roberts, Richard Ross, and Bryan Smith. *The Fifth Discipline Field Book: Strategies and Tools for Building a Learning Organization*. NY: Currency Doubleday, 1994.

Simons, George F. *Working Together, Third Edition*. Boston, MA: Thomson Learning/Course Technology, 2003.

Theobold, Robert. *The Rapids of Change*. Brookline, MA: Knowledge Press, 1988.

Tichy, Noel and Mary Ann Devanna. *The Transformational Manager*. NY: John Wiley & Sons, 1987.

84

NOTES

845-
0197

Tom

V.P.
(Premis in Nashville)

679-340-9000

V.P.

Butch Smith